Mad About Markers

WRITTEN BY
GRACE TAI

Walter Foster™

ILLUSTRATED BY
DIANA FISHER

The Fun Has Begun

This book brings the fun of markers to you,
with lots of ideas for making pictures too.
You don't need an eraser or pencil to start,
just colorful markers to create works of art!

Inside a marker is a wick dipped in ink.
It dries very fast, before you can blink!
Unlike a pencil, which you can erase,
once you draw a line, it stays in its place.

To make sure your ink doesn't get sapped,
those you're not using always keep capped.
Then find some paper that's smooth and white
It will make your colors look clean and bright.

Stay away from paper that's colored or rough,
for bringing out colors will be quite tough.
If you want to find paper that works the best,
check out some art stores from east to west!

HEY, CRAZY KIDS!
I'M FREDDY THE FROG!
LET'S MOSEY INTO
MARKER MANIA!

Your Cool Tools

How many markers do you need to draw?
As few as eight, but there's really no law!
A rainbow of colors you'll certainly need,
And an *indelible* marker that will not bleed.

medium

Points can be wide, medium, or thin,
fat like a brush or tiny like a pin!
See how many kinds of lines can appear?
Try not to touch them, or they might smear.

fine

wide

paint brush

indelible

Color Mixing Tricks

Everyone knows if you have a color or two,
you can mix them for others that are totally new!
Look to the left for a simple color wheel,
showing how to mix colors however you feel.

Blue and red for purple, blue and yellow for green.
Then check out this page for colors in between!
If you want to mix colors with your felt-tip markers,
use the light color first, then add what is darker!

A Parade of Shades

Do the colors shown here seem somehow related?
Some look brighter while others look faded.
Pick just one color—maybe red, purple, or green;
then lay down all of the shades in between.

Try dark and light shades with all sorts of blues.
Below you'll find more of what we call *hues*.
Notice that these shades don't really contrast
but make a cool dinosaur scene from the past.

White Is Outta Sight

Markers, you see, come in colors light and bright,
but you can't ever buy them in just plain white.
To get some white things to take shape and be seen,
leave those spots on your paper totally clean.

Try objects you know, like trees, fish, or hearts.
It's neat to watch shapes transform into art.

See how some objects really stand out?
Yellow on blue makes the star really shout!
The pale blue shape seems to fade away fast,
so use opposite shades for *color contrast.*

Be a Champ with Stamps

Here's a way to make your art really shout.
Follow these steps for some stamps to try out.
The first thing you need is a Styrofoam™ tray.
Cut out an object in a neat shape or way.

Press hard with a pen to inscribe a design.
Glue a handle on back to hold it just fine.
Color the stamp with any marker you desire.
Push it down on the paper, stand back, and admire!

Giggles of Squiggles

Has anyone ever told you this secret before?
You can use squiggly lines for pictures galore!
Blobs, splashes, and spots—feel free to splurge.
Color around them, and watch objects emerge.

Use doodles to draw anything you wish.
Turn squiggles into a bright, wiggly fish.
You'll find this method lets you draw with speed.
Make an underwater world with slimy seaweed!

Outlines Are Fine

Art is so easy, and soon you will find
you can make pictures with simple outlines.
Draw your shapes with a marker black and thin,
then pick out some colors to fill them all in.

To fill in the sun and make it look true,
use orange inside the circle you drew.
Be careful as you let the marker glide.
You don't want any color to slip outside!

Lines in one direction appear smooth like below.
Then draw the other way, so the white doesn't show.
Work very slowly with great artistic skill.
The finished picture will produce a great thrill!

LET YOUR LINES LOOSE!

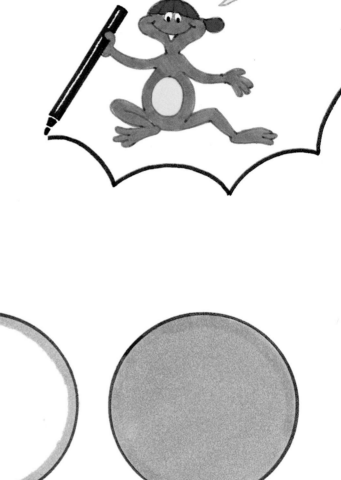

Lots of Dots

It's fun to make pictures using bunches of dots,
like a cool outdoor scene with a sun looking hot!
When drawing with dots, it's also no doubt,
you can place them close or very spread out.

Just as you've learned, outline the shape first.
Then fill it with dots 'til it's ready to burst!
It's fun to line them up in neat swirls and trails
for drawing waves or slow-moving snails.

Another way to give your dot drawings some zip
is to use lots of markers with different size tips.
Your drawings depend on what you can dream,
a hippo, a rainbow, or drippy ice cream!

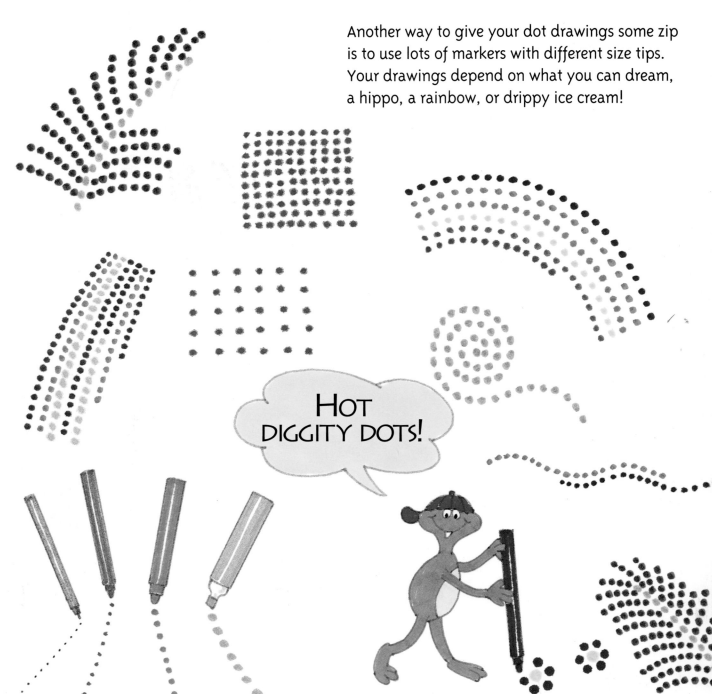

HOT DIGGITY DOTS!

Drawing Lines that Shine

You can also use a long trustworthy line
to make circles, squares, and triangles fine.
The closer your lines, the darker your shade.
Draw them spaced out, and the color will fade.

To keep your objects from looking too flat,
combine lines with markers thin, medium, and fat.
Put them together, creating all sorts of shapes,
and you can end up with a crazy landscape!

A Fun Lecture on Texture

Practice drawing all these fine examples to learn
how textures emerge from a simple pattern.
Make lines that curve down the small lizard's tail.
Add a pattern of swirls to give it some scales.

Use stripes, slashes, or zigzagging strokes
to draw a cactus with sharp pricklies that poke.
Patches and streaks will look super keen
when you turn them into a hot desert scene!

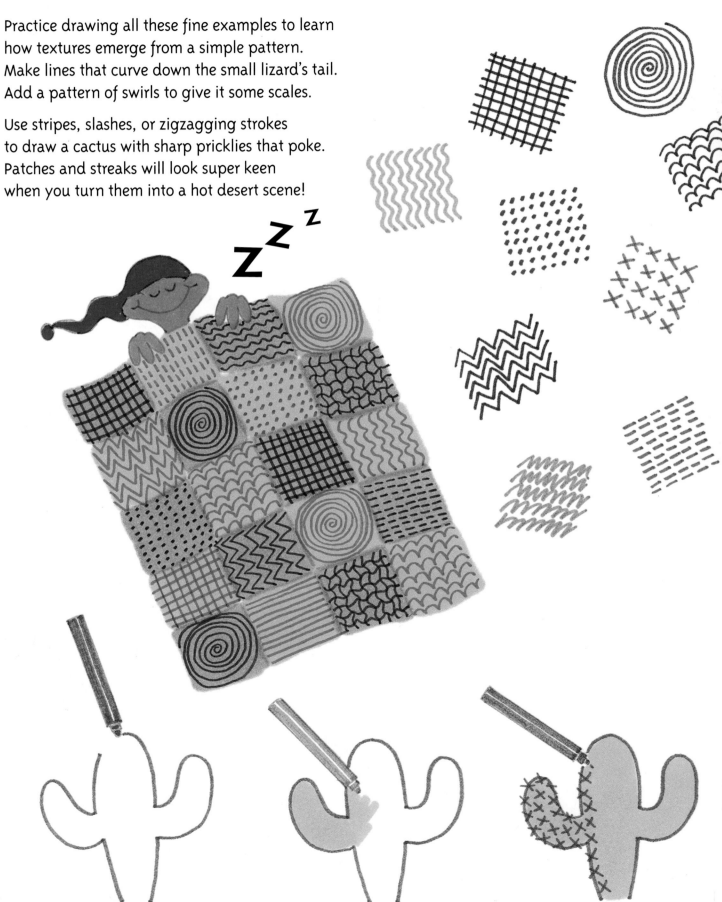

Dare to Be A Square

Those triangles, circles, and squares you know well
can be put together for a drawing that's swell.
Pick shapes you like, and connect their sides.
Turn them 'to cows that give children fun rides.

SNAPPY SHAPES MAKE ME SMILE!

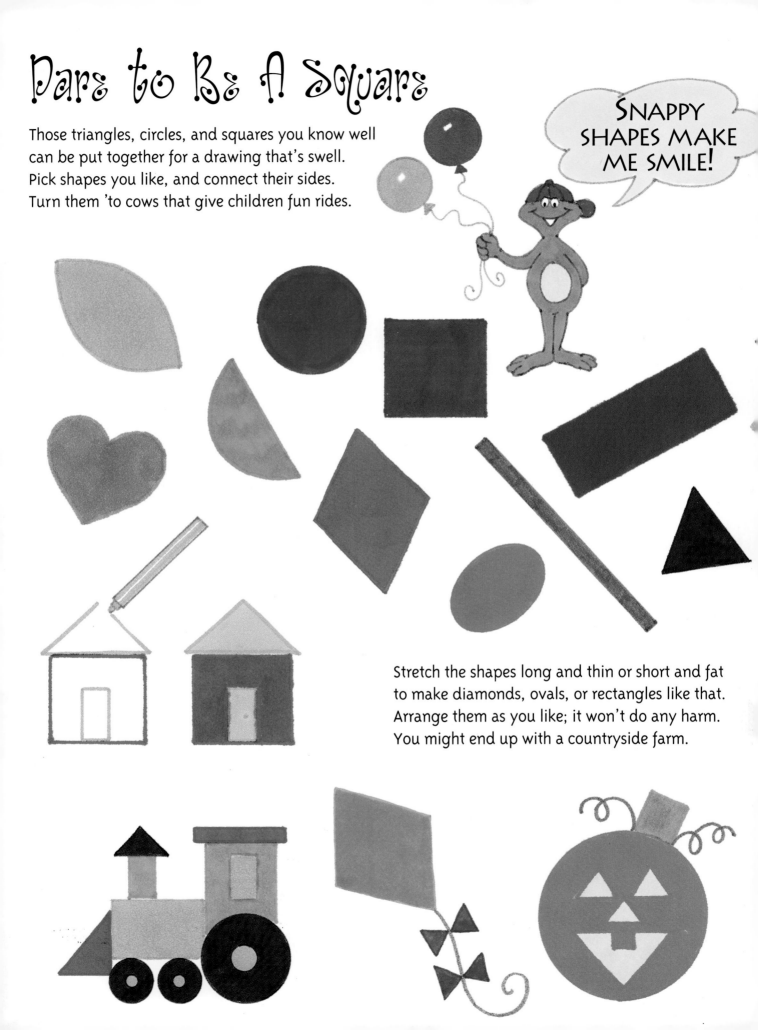

Stretch the shapes long and thin or short and fat
to make diamonds, ovals, or rectangles like that.
Arrange them as you like; it won't do any harm.
You might end up with a countryside farm.

The Chase to Trace

You can take objects with any shape or surface
and trace around them for an artistic purpose.
The first thing to do is to search and to roam
for objects you can locate outside or at home.

Find leaves, buttons, or cans you can test.
Trace them to get the shapes that work best.
Lay your hand flat, and don't let it wobble.
Trace a turkey that shouts, "Hey, gobble, gobble!"

Trace your own foot to create a happy giraffe
or a dispenser of tape to make an elephant laugh.
Put the shapes together for an entire work of art.
When it's all finished, you'll feel really smart!

Black Is Back

It's fun to create an outer space scene
with shiny spaceships and bright stars that beam.
The best way to keep this drawing on track
is to make great use of the marker that's black.

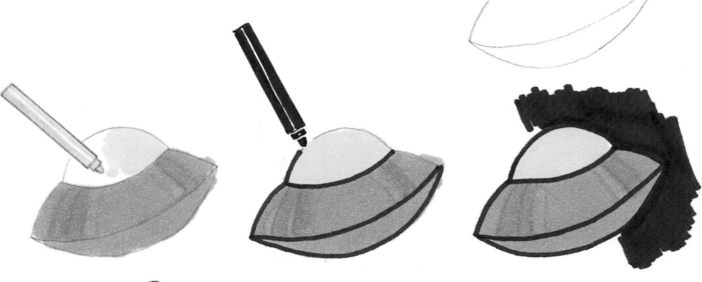

Sketch shapes of your objects, use a pencil this time.
Then fill them in with bright colors you find.
Use the black marker; fill the space all around.
Don't color the shapes—just the background.

Elation with Gradation

It's exciting to use colors for special effects.
You don't need spots, stripes, or tiny specks.
Use markers to color from lightest to darkest,
and you will become a most excellent artist.

Fill in your shapes with this kind of technique
for a picture of butterflies playing Hide 'n' Seek.
Once you've learned how to apply *gradation,*
you should give yourself a standing ovation!

GO GAGA FOR GRADATION!

Letters Get Better

It's probably a pretty good guess or hunch
that you like to write your name a whole bunch.
So when using markers, it's surely a treat
to make your writing look wonderfully neat!

HAPPY

COOL!

rainbow

slime

Shadow

Shadow

Since letters have many little shapes inside,
you can fill them with any color you decide.
Another way to make your writing shine
is to add a cool shadow or color outline.

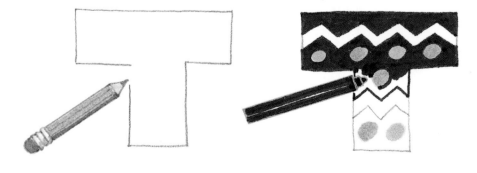

Practice all the examples we have shown,
then try to come up with some of your own!

High Regard for Cards

It's certainly obvious and we hope you agree
that markers will help you make cards easily.
If you like to give people wishes or greetings,
make them a card that will send hearts a' fleeting.

Take a thick piece of paper, and fold it in half.
Write a message inside that will make a friend laugh.
With drawings and shapes that you have compiled,
your card will no doubt produce some big smiles.

With markers, you see, there's no end to the fun.
You can be proud of all you have done!
And even though you've found the very last page,
keep on drawing 'til you reach a ripe old age!